/07

Career Assessments and Their Meanings

CAREERS WITH CHARACTER

Careers with Character

Career Assessments and Their Meanings

by Ellyn Sanna

MASON CREST PUBLISHERS

Mason Crest Publishers Inc.
370 Reed Road, Broomall, Pennsylvania 19008
(866) MCP-BOOK (toll free)
www.masoncrest.com

First edition, 2003
13 12 11 10 09 08 07 06 05   10 9 8 7 6 5 4 3 2

Library of Congress Cataloging-in-Publication Data

Sanna, Ellyn, 1958-
Career assessments and their meanings / by Ellyn Sanna.
p. cm.—(Careers with character)
Summary: Explains how assessment procedures can assist in finding the profession
that is best suited to one's personality and talents. Includes bibliographical references
and index.
    ISBN   1-59084-309-6
           1-59084-327-4 (series)
1. Student aspirations—Handbooks, manuals, etc.—Juvenile literature. 2. Vocational
guidance—Handbooks, manuals, etc.—Juvenile literature. 3. Career development—
Handbooks, manuals, etc.—Juvenile literature.
[1. Vocational guidance—Handbooks, manuals, etc. 2. Career development—
Handbooks, manuals, etc.]
I. Title. II. Series.
 LB1027.8.S26 2003
 372'.01'13—dc21

Design by Lori Holland.
Composition by Bytheway Publishing Services, Binghamton, New York.
Printed in the Hashemite Kingdom of Jordan.

Photo Credits:
Comstock: pp. 4, 74, 77, 80
Corbis: cover
PhotoDisc: pp. 14, 16, 24, 29, 36, 38, 41, 44, 46, 52, 54, 57, 60, 62, 66, 68

CONTENTS

We each leave a fingerprint on the world.
Our careers are the work we do in life.
Our characters are shaped by the choices
we make to do good.
When we combine careers with character,
we touch the world with power.

INTRODUCTION

by Dr. Cheryl Gholar
and Dr. Ernestine G. Riggs

In today's world, the awesome task of choosing or staying in a career has become more involved than one would ever have imagined in past decades. Whether the job market is robust or the demand for workers is sluggish, the need for top-performing employees with good character remains a priority on most employers' lists of "must have" or "must keep." When critical decisions are being made regarding a company or organization's growth or future, job performance and work ethic are often the determining factors as to who will remain employed and who will not.

How does one achieve success in one's career and in life? Victor Frankl, the Austrian psychologist, summarized the concept of success in the preface to his book *Man's Search for Meaning* as: "The unintended side-effect of one's personal dedication to a course greater than oneself." Achieving value by responding to life and careers from higher levels of knowing and being is a specific goal of teaching and learning in "Careers with Character." What constitutes success for us as individuals can be found deep within our belief system. Seeking, preparing, and attaining an excellent career that aligns with our personality is an outstanding goal. However, an excellent career augmented by exemplary character is a visible expression of the human need to bring meaning, purpose, and value to our work.

Career education informs us of employment opportunities, occupational outlooks, earnings, and preparation needed to perform certain

1

tasks. Character education provides insight into how a person of good character might choose to respond, initiate an action, or perform specific tasks in the presence of an ethical dilemma. "Careers with Character" combines the two and teaches students that careers are more than just jobs. Career development is incomplete without character development. What better way to explore careers and character than to make them a single package to be opened, examined, and reflected upon as a means of understanding the greater whole of who we are and what work can mean when one chooses to become an employee of character?

Character can be defined simply as "who you are even when no one else is around." Your character is revealed by your choices and actions. These bear your personal signature, validating the story of who you are. They are the fingerprints you leave behind on the people you meet and know; they are the ideas you bring into reality. Your choices tell the world what you truly believe.

Character, when viewed as a standard of excellence, reminds us to ask ourselves when choosing a career: "Why this particular career, for what purpose, and to what end?" The authors of "Careers with Character" knowledgeably and passionately, through their various vignettes, enable one to experience an inner journey that is both intellectual and moral. Students will find themselves, when confronting decisions in real life, more prepared, having had experiential learning opportunities through this series. The books, however, do not separate or negate the individual good from the academic skills or intellect needed to perform the required tasks that lead to productive career development and personal fulfillment.

Each book is replete with exemplary role models, practical strategies, instructional tools, and applications. In each volume, individuals of character work toward ethical leadership, learning how to respond appropriately to issues of not only right versus wrong, but issues of right versus right, understanding the possible benefits and consequences of their decisions. A wealth of examples is provided.

What is it about a career that moves our hearts and minds toward fulfilling a dream? It is our character. The truest approach to finding out who we are and what illuminates our lives is to look within. At the very heart of career development is good character. At the heart of good character is an individual who knows and loves the good, and seeks to share the good with others. By exploring careers and character together, we create internal and external environments that support and enhance each other, challenging students to lead conscious lives of personal quality and true richness every day.

Is there a difference between doing the right thing, and doing things right? Career questions ask, "What do you know about a specific career?" Character questions ask, "Now that you know about a specific career, what will you choose to do with what you know?" "How will you perform certain tasks and services for others, even when no one else is around?" "Will all individuals be given your best regardless of their socioeconomic background, physical condition, ethnicity, or religious beliefs?" Character questions often challenge the authenticity of what we say we believe and value in the workplace and in our personal lives.

Character and career questions together challenge us to pay attention to our lives and not fall asleep on the job. Career knowledge, self-knowledge, and ethical wisdom help us answer deeper questions about the meaning of work; they give us permission to transform our lives. Personal integrity is the price of admission.

The insight of one "ordinary" individual can make a difference in the world—if that one individual believes that character is an amazing gift to uncap knowledge and talents to empower the human community. Our world needs everyday heroes in the workplace—and "Careers with Character" challenges students to become those heroes.

Deciding which career door to open and enter is one of the most important decisions you will ever make in your life.

1

CHOOSING A CAREER

*Some people know what they want to be
from the time they are children . . .
while for others, determining their
career is a lifelong process.*

Sara England was confused. Her senior year of high school was fast approaching—and she still didn't know what she wanted to do after graduation. All her friends seemed so certain about their plans for the years ahead. Many of them had already been accepted at the college they wanted to attend; most of them had their major, minor, and future profession all mapped. Not everyone she knew was going to college, of course: one friend would be working in his father's hardware store; another friend was joining the Peace Corps for two years; but everyone knew what they would be doing two years from now and they were eagerly moving ahead with their lives. Only Sara had no idea where she was going.

She was pretty sure she wanted to go to college—but she didn't know what degree she should work toward, and so she didn't know *which* college would be best for her to attend. For a while when she was younger she had wanted to be a veterinarian, and she still loved taking care of animals—but she didn't enjoy studying math and science, and she had learned that these subjects would be important for a degree in veterinarian medicine. Besides, she wasn't sure if her grades would be good enough for her to be accepted into a veterinarian program. That career sounded like too much work, and she had pretty much given up on the idea.

But she didn't know what else to focus on instead. She was fairly certain she didn't want to do anything that involved computers or math—but she didn't know what she *would* like to do. What if her parents paid all that money for her to go to college . . . and by the end of the four years, she still didn't know what she wanted to do? Maybe it would be better for her to get a job at the local department store until she could figure out what interested her. But what if nothing ever came along to help her make up her mind—and she ended up spending her whole life in a job that didn't thrill her?

The more Sara thought about the years ahead, the more confused she felt. If she could at least decide on which step to take next, maybe the other steps would fall in place as she went. But she didn't have a clue about even that first step. She needed someone—or something—to help her make this important decision in her life.

That's what career **assessment** measures are designed to do: they help individuals determine which career would be best suited to their particular skills and interests. The results from these techniques help people map out plans for their professional lives. These assessment tools do this in two ways: first, by helping individuals understand what's *out there* in the real-life job world, and second, by helping individuals better understand what's *inside* them, as far as skills and interests.

The first step in this two-pronged process is to gather as much information as possible. Information is made up of facts, and these are important for giving us a foundation on which to build our sense of what work we would be best suited to do in life. Here are examples of information we need to know in order to build a career plan:

- Projected characteristics of the job market for the next ten years.
- Salary ranges for various occupations.
- Education needed for particular jobs.

- Which colleges or universities offer which programs.
- The cost of tuition at various colleges or universities.
- Personal talents or skills.
- Personal interests.
- Personality qualities and how these will better suit us for one job over another.
- Character qualities and how we can use these to build our careers.

Gathering information is an important step in the career assessment process. Some people, however, may be more comfortable with this stage of the process than they are with the ones that follow. The temptation may be to remain at this stage, gathering more and more information and never moving on to a decision. However, no matter how many facts we gather, there will always be gaps in our information, things we cannot know or predict. Information has its limitations.

Ultimately, information alone will not be enough for us to make a career decision. According to Richard N. Bolles, coauthor of *The Career Counselor's Handbook,* we need to take *information* a step higher and turn it into *knowledge.* Knowledge is different from information, says Bolles, because it is organized and applied.

In other words, knowledge is information that has been organized into headings that make sense to our own situations. Instead of having merely a vast collection of facts, career assessment helps us break those facts down into the answers to these three questions:

1. What do I most want to do?
2. Where do I want to do it?
3. How can I gain the requirements I need to do it?

As we organize our information into categories that apply to our own situation, "knowledge" also helps us apply that information in practical ways. We learn what steps to take next. We understand the details of what concrete actions must be taken, and we realize the sequential order in which to take them.

Ideally, however, the knowledge we gain from career assessment needs to be taken yet one more level higher. According to Bolles, wisdom is the next step up from knowledge. Wisdom helps us place our knowledge in a larger, less self-centered context. We come to see our place in our community and in our world—and this new larger perspective helps us to see the true importance of various elements in our lives.

For instance, we may be preoccupied with salary. If so, all the information we gather will tend to focus on money:

How much would a particular college program cost?
How much money can we expect to make in a particular career?
What would be the entry-level salary?
How quickly can we expect to get raises?

As we organize and apply this information, gaining knowledge, we may still be obsessed with finances. But as we put this knowledge into a larger context, gaining wisdom, we may begin to see that money is not as important as we had first thought. Meanwhile, as money's importance in our lives changes, other factors may take on new prominence. We may realize we would be willing to do a job we love for less money—and we may also come to understand that no amount of money is worth doing certain jobs that drain the joy from our lives.

> Starting out to make money is the greatest mistake in life. Do what you feel you have a flair for doing, and if you are good enough at it, the money will come.
> —Greer Garson

You can begin now to collect information on careers and job opportunities—and in the months ahead, you can begin to sort this information into a strong knowledge base . . . and eventually you will arrive at the wisdom you need to make choices about your future. The following list contains some places where you might begin your search for information.

Personal Contacts

Your family and friends may be more helpful than you might at first think. Ask as many people as you can about the careers that interest you. You may find your friends and family either already know the answers to your questions—or they can put you in touch with someone else who does. This is a good technique for gathering information about a specific career or company, and you may gain inside information and other helpful hints about the type of training necessary for a certain position. You can also find out how people in that position entered the field, the prospects for advancement, and what they like and dislike about the work.

Public Libraries

You may be surprised to find your local library has a great deal of up-to-date career material. To begin your library search, look at listings under "vocations" or "careers" and then under specific fields. Check the periodical section, where you'll find trade and professional magazines and journals about specific occupations and industries. You can become familiar with the concerns and activities of potential employers by skimming their annual reports and other public documents. You might also want to check out occupational information on videos, computer programs, or programs available through the Internet. Don't forget the librarians, who can be a great source that can save you valuable time by directing you to relevant information.

Internet Resources

The Internet gives you access to countless resources instantly at any time. Most companies, professional societies, academic institutions, and government agencies maintain Internet sites where you can find the organization's latest information and activities. Listings may include information such as government documents, schedules of events, and job openings. Listings for academic institutions often provide links to career counseling and placement services through career resource centers, as well as information on financing your education. Colleges and universities also offer on-line guides to campus facilities and admission requirements and procedures.

The variety of career information available through the Internet provides much of the same information available through libraries, career centers, and guidance offices. However, no single network or resource will contain all the information you need, so be prepared to search in a variety of places. As in a library search, look through various lists by field or discipline, or by using keywords.

Career sites can be an excellent place to obtain information about job opportunities. They provide a forum for employers to list job openings and for individuals to post their resumes. Some Internet sites may also provide an opportunity to research a particular industry or company. For instance, America's Career InfoNet provides a wealth of information for anyone exploring different careers. It provides data on employment growth and wages by occupation; the knowledge, skills, and abilities required for a particular occupation; and links to employers. America's Job Bank (AJB), administered by the U.S. Department of Labor, is another good site for you to check. On any given day, it lists as many as a million job openings across the United States. (For still more career sites available on the Internet, read chapter 7.)

Career Centers, and Guidance Offices

Check your school's career centers for resources such as individual counseling and testing, guest speakers, field trips, books, career magazines, and career days. The centers usually will have professionals who are trained to help you discover your strengths and weaknesses, evaluate your goals and values, and help you determine what career would best suit you. Counselors should not tell you what to do—but they may administer interest inventories and aptitude tests, interpret the results, and help you explore various options. Counselors also may discuss local job markets and the ***entry requirements***, and they can help you discover the costs of schools, colleges, or training programs.

The *Dictionary of Occupational Titles*, published by the U.S. Department of Labor, lists more than 20,000 different job-titles. The Department of Labor breaks these jobs down into 19 families:

1. Managerial and Management-Related Occupations
2. Engineers, Surveyors, and Architects
3. Natural, Computer, and Mathematical Scientists
4. Lawyers, Social Scientists, Social Workers, and Religious Workers
5. Teachers, Librarians, and Counselors
6. Health Diagnosing and Treating Practitioners
7. Registered Nurses, Pharmacists, Dieticians, Therapists, and Physician Assistants
8. Health Technologies and Technicians
9. Writers, Artists, and Entertainers
10. Technologists and Technicians, Other Than Health
11. Marketing and Sales Occupations
12. Administrative Support Occupations, Including Clerical
13. Service Occupations
14. Agriculture, Forestry, Fishing, and Related Occupations
15. Mechanics, Installers, and Repairers
16. Construction Trades and Extractive Occupations
17. Production Occupations
18. Transportation and Material Moving Occupations
19. Handlers, Equipment Cleaners, Helpers, and Laborers

Whatever sources you use to gather information, don't just blindly swallow everything you hear. Assess career guidance materials carefully. You need information that is current and objective. Watch out for materials that seem to glamorize the occupation, overstate the earnings, or exaggerate the demand for workers. Use your common sense.

Career assessments can help you begin the process from information to knowledge to wisdom. They can certainly help you know which

Changing Career Concepts

Your concept of "career" probably isn't the same as your grandparents'. In today's changing world, people no longer look at their work in the same way as they did a generation ago.

The Old Career Model: The Step Ladder

1. Career grows because of **tenure** and performance.
2. Career follows a linear, one-direction path.
3. The path moves progressively higher in prestige, power, and pay.
4. The ideal path begins and ends with a single, long-term employer.
5. Career focuses on particular strengths and competencies.

The New Career Model: The Spiral

1. Career grows because of wide and varied experiences.
2. Career follows a **cyclical** and twisting path.
3. The path generally stays at one level as it moves from place to place.
4. The ideal path will entail multiple relationships with a number of employers.
5. Career focuses on several growing, ever-developing strengths and competencies.

Adapted from the Institute for the Future, Career Revisited, Outlook Project, 1997.

step to take next to begin. For most of us, however, wisdom cannot be gained from simply taking a test, reading a *trade journal*, or talking with a guidance counselor. Although career assessment techniques may help point us in the right direction, gaining the wisdom we need to evaluate our life's career will be a long process. For some it may even take years.

For instance, Sara England spent some time in her high school guidance office taking some of the many career assessment tests her counselor offered—and she gained important information about herself and the work world. Her guidance counselor helped her sort that information and apply it to her own life. Based on the knowledge she has gained, Sara has decided to apply to a four-year college that offers a wide-based liberal arts program. She has selected several colleges that will offer her what she needs, and she knows what she should do next to submit her applications. But Sara doesn't have her entire life plan all mapped.

Instead, she has gained just enough wisdom to understand she doesn't have all the answers yet. Although she would like to have definite goals to work toward like her friends, she understands now that some people need more time to determine what they want to do in life. In the larger context of life, she realizes, being happy and doing well on the stage where you're at in the present is more important than claiming a lofty goal for the future.

Some people may already know exactly what's inside them as far as interests and aptitudes and they may be well aware of how they want to apply that to the world of work. Sara needs a little more time, though. Along the way, she plans to avail herself of other career assessment measures to help her better understand both herself and the work world. She's looking forward to her college years—and she plans to explore lots of options so she can decide the next stage of her career journey.

First say to yourself what you would be, and then do what you have to do.

—Epictetus

Understanding yourself is one of the first steps toward choosing a career path to follow.

2

ASSESSING YOURSELF

You have to know who you are before
you can know what you want.

Like Sara England, Josh Hardy isn't sure what career he wants to pursue. He's not certain what he really wants out of life.

Up until recently, however, he was certain he wanted to be a doctor. Ever since he was a little boy, this had been his career goal, and it had seemed to make perfect sense. After all, he enjoyed math and science, which would be important if he were to major in pre-med in college. His father was a doctor as well, and Josh was familiar with the demands and rewards of a doctor's lifestyle.

During his senior year of high school, though, his father got him an after-school job at the local hospital. Josh ran errands, helped out with filing and other clerical jobs, and spent time with patients. To his surprise, he found himself dreading going in to the hospital each day.

He hated the smell there. He wasn't good at talking with the patients. The very sight of illness and pain depressed him. The sense of urgency and tension that filled the hallways made him feel anxious and tense.

Josh has already been accepted into a pre-med program for next year, and he knows his father is excited about his son following in his footsteps. But Josh keeps thinking about something his grandmother used to say to him: "Be careful what you wish for—because you might just get it." As a child, he always used to think it was a stupid saying; after all, why wouldn't you want whatever you wished for? Now, though, he's beginning to understand what his grandmother meant.

But what can he do? He's ashamed to admit to his family and friends that he hates the hospital atmosphere. Maybe, he worries, his feelings indicate he's a weak person. If he just pushes himself to move forward toward a career as a doctor, perhaps he'll get over his silly anxieties and depression.

Josh decides to go talk to his guidance counselor. He hopes she can help him see things more clearly.

Understanding what's really important to you is one of the important aspects of career assessment. There's nothing wrong with being unclear about what you want most in life; in fact, it's a normal part of everyone's life journey. It takes time and careful thought to understand yourself better. Career assessment measures can't give you magic solutions

Talking with a guidance counselor or other career counselor can often help you gain understanding of yourself.

Most career counselors believe gathering information about your own interests is a key first step in determining the right career for you. Some interests may change with time, while other core interests will remain stable. An important part of understanding your interests is determining which interests are basic parts of your personality—and which aren't.

For instance, are you interested in sports at this point in your life merely because of the opportunity for social interaction sports events provide—or is your interest in sports an enduring part of your personality, one around which you might shape a successful career? Ten years from now, do you think you will still like playing computer games? If the answer is yes, then you might find computer programming for a company that develops games a fulfilling career. But if the answer is no, you need to find another more enduring interest around which to shape your future work life.

to your future, like shaking an Eight-Ball, but they are designed to give you tools to help you understand yourself better.

From your performance in school, you may already have a good idea what you're good at, but career assessment measures can help you fine-tune that information. They can aid you as you sort it into knowledge that applies to your career life, and they can help you gain the wisdom you need to put your skills, personality, and character in a larger context.

Each of us enters the work world with a unique package to offer. Our individual skills and personalities are an enormous part of these packages. Our characters are another.

Our personalities are shaped by both our environment and our **genetic** heredity. It's that old nurture/nature thing you may have learned about in science class. To some extent you are who you are because of the specific characteristics you have inherited from your biological parents. Along with your mother's blue eyes and your father's long legs,

> The greatest achievement of the human spirit is to live up to one's opportunities and make the most of one's resources.
> —Vauvenargues

you may have gotten your aptitude for languages from your mother and your quick temper from your father. The environment in which you grew then shaped and built on these inherited qualities, creating the person you are today. Choosing the career that's right for you will depend in part on understanding that entire package that makes up your personality.

Character is something a bit different. While you may have little control over the forces that shaped your personality, you can *choose* the sort of character you want to have. Character is built on the decisions you make about right and wrong, about what is most important in your life, and about what the real meaning of work is. According to experts in character education like Tom Lickona and Michael Josephson, a good character is built on possessing certain core qualities such as these:

- integrity and trustworthiness
- compassion and respect for others
- justice and fairness
- responsibility
- courage
- self-discipline and diligence
- citizenship

Only you can decide whether you want these core qualities to be a part of your daily life—both today and in whatever career you choose for the future.

In the chapters that follow, we will look at several specific career assessment tests that can help you better understand your personality and what you do best. In the past, as career counselors helped individuals better understand themselves, they focused mainly on this aspect of self-awareness. Recently, however, career counselors have come to appreciate that character issues are an important part of choosing the career that's right for you.

Understanding what we value most is an essential part of the career decision-making process. According to career counselors Mark Guterman and Terry Karp, "values" all have this in common:

- *They are guiding principles in life.* They answer the question, "What is most important to me?"
- *They are not situational.* In other words, our values are the guiding principles that shape who we are in both work and nonwork situations; they do not change from one setting to another.
- *They influence decisions and actions.* They help us choose both work and nonwork activities that are meaningful.
- *Values can be prioritized.* You can sort out which values are most important to you and which have less bearing on your life.

Career counselors use a variety of techniques to help individuals gather information, knowledge, and wisdom about their values. One of these, a set of cards called *ValueSearch,* will be discussed in more detail

Your skills and talents are important information for determining your career. These aptitudes will help you see where you function most comfortably. Examples of these skills include:

- muscle coordination
- manual dexterity
- the ability to visualize things in three dimensions
- verbal communication skills
- the ability to work well with the written language
- mathematical ability
- musical talent
- artistic skills

Aptitudes like these do not come and go; they will remain with you for your entire life.

Career assessment needs to combine both your interests and your talents. For instance, on a particular test, an individual may score high on areas that indicate he would work well with paperwork. His paperwork efficiency, however, may not mean he should become a clerical worker—not if he has no interest in this kind of work. Instead, he needs to continue the assessment process to determine a career where he can use his skill in a way that interests him.

in chapter 9. Other less formal assessment measures can also be useful.

For instance, journaling can be an important tool in the career counseling process. As you keep a journal, you can gain awareness of what matters most to you. One technique for applying the core character qualities to your own life is to write an imaginary dialogue with them. For instance, you might write a conversation between you and "integrity." Don't try to judge what you are saying as you write; simply put down whatever comes to mind. There are no "right" answers.

Here's one set of questions that might help you see what's most important to you:

- When you look back at the last week, what things seem the most important to you? (Emotions, events, relationships, achievements, etc.)
- What things did you enjoy most?
- What things did you do best?
- In what settings are you most comfortable? (Informal/formal, alone/with people, outdoors/indoors, etc.)
- What things would you like to do again?
- Is there anything you did in the last week you would like to still be doing (in some shape or form) ten years from now?

Your goal is simply to understand yourself better.

Another technique career counselors sometimes use is a lifeline. A lifeline is similar to the timelines you may have created for history class—except your personal lifeline will indicate the "defining moments" in your individual life. As you look back on your life, what are the particular events or decisions that were most important to who you are today? The counselor can help you explore the underlying themes and styles revealed by your lifeline.

All these techniques are designed to help you better understand who you are and what is most important to you. In today's world, you probably won't be able to separate work from the rest of your life. As computers and the Internet allow many jobs to be done anywhere, any time, the boundaries between work and life become increasingly blurred. As a result, more and more people who think about careers and work are coming to realize we need a **holistic** approach to career planning. You need to consider your social, emotional, intellectual, and even spiritual needs as you decide on which career is best for you.

In Josh Hardy's case, this means he needs to pay attention to who he is. If he takes time to decide what he is good at, what he enjoys most, and what is most important to

> ### Determining What's Most Important
>
> If life were a pie, how would you divide it into pieces?
>
> List the things in your life that are important to you. Then draw a circle and give each item on your list the size piece you want it to have in your life.

> Make a list of what you love to do. Here are some possible examples:
>
> - cooking
> - listening to music
> - being with friends
> - reading
> - watching sports events
> - shopping
> - spending time in nature
> - being alone
>
> After you've written your list, think about what careers would offer you the most chances to do the things you like best.

him, he will have a better sense of the direction he should take in the years ahead.

After spending time with his guidance counselor, Josh decides to give himself more time to get used to the hospital environment. However, he's thinking a career in medical research might suit him better than a career as a doctor. As he discusses the results of his career assessments with his parents and the guidance counselor, they all agree that research looks like an ideal field for Josh.

The career counselor helped Josh understand *who he is*, in terms of personality. Only Josh, however, can decide *who he wants to be*, in terms of character. Remember the old question adults always ask children: "What do you want to be when you grow up?" You've reached the point in your life where you can finally decide on the answer. Counselors, friends, and parents can help you as you make the decision, but ultimately, it's up to you.

What's right for you might not be right for anyone else, but that doesn't matter. Take the time to get to know yourself. Once you do, you can start to explore the options that lie waiting in the world of work.

Follow your bliss. Find where it is and don't be afraid to follow it.

—Joseph Campbell

Right now your attention may be fixed on one goal—graduation—but once you've reached that exciting achievement, what will you do next?

3

ASSESSING THE WORK WORLD

*Determine the facts—and then see how you
can use them to reach your goals.*

Ever since Terrell Washington was a little boy he's loved spending time on his grandfather's farm. He likes watching things grow; he enjoys working with farm animals; and he wants to leave the city behind and live his life connected more closely to the Earth's seasonal rhythms. "I'm going to be a farmer when I grow up," he has always insisted.

But as a high school student, Terrell has begun to suspect his dream is just not practical. He doesn't know anyone else who plans on becoming a farmer after graduation, and he knows more and more farmers face serious financial problems.

Terrell's not sure what he should do. Should he consider his life-long dream to be a part of childhood he needs to leave behind? Or is there a way he can fit his passion for farming into today's work world? Terrell has learned a lot from his grandfather about farming—but his grandfather can't seem to help him when it comes to finding the answers he needs.

The world of work has changed drastically since Terrell's grandfather entered it. The old man is wise enough to know that a guidance counselor or career counselor can help Terrell more than he can. Terrell needs to gain information about today's work world—and a counselor

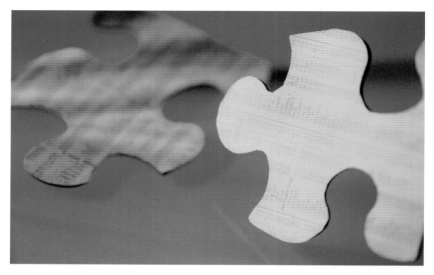

Finding out information about the work world will help you fill in some missing pieces as you puzzle out what to do with your life.

can help him convert that information into knowledge that applies to his own situation. Based on that knowledge base, Terrell can then find the wisdom he needs to plan his future career.

Today's employment environment is far different from the one that existed even 20 years ago. Employees' expectations are different, and so are employers'. Ever-developing technology is changing our world at a pace that is faster than ever before in history, and this trend affects not only our personal lives but our professional ones as well. One result of all this new technology is that we live in a world that is increasingly global in focus; the Internet means companies can do business around the world 24 hours a day. Another result is that workers will need to possess new skills.

    The work world Terrell will soon enter is in the midst of a revolution—the Information Revolution. Just as the Industrial Revolution created enormous changes in the lives of human beings during the 19th century, today's revolution is changing the way we all live—and especially the way we work.

The Information Revolution means we live in a world where the economy is increasingly based on some form of knowledge, whether processes, skills, technologies, or information about customers and suppliers. Industries that transport information are growing faster than those that transport goods. (According to T.A. Stewart's book, *Intellectual Capital*, voice telephone usage has been increasing at a rate of 16 percent a year, data traffic has increased at about 30 percent per year, and the Internet has grown still faster.) Companies today no longer have to carry inventory; instead, through the Internet or phone system, customers can place an order, the company passes it along to the manufacturer via the Internet, and the product is shipped directly to the customer. The volume of on-line business doubles every 100 days.

How will this revolution affect the work world? It will mean that professionals like lawyers, engineers, and teachers will no longer be the only ones who deal with information. Instead, some skill in this area will be required of nearly everyone. For instance, there are very few

In the 21st century, the expectations between employees and employers has changed.

Old Expectations	New Expectations
stability, predictability	change, uncertainty
permanency	temporariness
standard work patterns	flexible work
loyalty	skills and performance more important
paternalism	self-reliance
job security	employment security
linear career growth	multiple careers
onetime learning	lifelong learning

As the 20th century began, most people in the United States and Canada made their living as farmers. By the middle of the century, more than 50 percent were employed in manufacturing jobs. Today, the majority of all workers are employed by companies that either deal with information or provide some sort of service for others.

jobs today where you are not expected to have at least some knowledge of how to use a computer. Conveying knowledge quickly from person to person will play an ever-increasing role in the job descriptions of many professions.

The work world is different today from what it was a generation ago in other ways as well. Today, more and more women are in the workforce. Since most women with professional lives are still mothers, they have helped create a work atmosphere that tends to be more open to flexible work hours and family demands; they are helping to bring a healthier balance between work and the "rest of life."

According to Andrea Saveri and Rod Falcon in their article "Planning for the 21st-Century Workforce" (*New Directions in Career Plan-*

A Global Marketplace

A single worldwide market has been created by factors like these:

- global telecommunications that rely on fiber optics, satellites, and computer technology
- giant multinational corporations that do business around the world
- growing free trade between the nations of the world
- 24-hour-a-day financial markets
- international investment among multinational companies ($315 billion in 1996 alone)
- new global standards and regulations for trade, commerce, finance, products, and services

ning and the Workplace), the many changes in today's work world have these implications:

- *Lifelong learning and skill development will be essential.* As occupations grow, they will demand higher levels of education and skills. Employees will need to constantly build their skills through continuing education and other experiences.
- *Workers should expect to have multiple careers.* At the same time that people are living longer because of improved medical technology, employers are offering fewer long-term positions. This means that many people will need to pursue second (and even third and fourth) careers.
- *Workers in any workforce will be spread across a wide age range.* Older individuals in the workplace will mean that younger workers have opportunities to learn from those who are more experienced, while older workers can benefit from the new generation's perspectives and creativity.

Your guidance counselor or librarian can direct you toward sources of information about the world of work.

Number of Jobs in Major Industry Sectors (Millions), 1986–2006

Year	Service Producing	Percent of Total	Goods Producing	Percent of Total
1986	74.2	63.0	24.5	20.8
1996	93.3	69.7	24.4	18.2
2006	111.9	75.2	24.5	16.5

Source: U.S. Bureau of the Census, *Statistical Abstract of the United States: 1998,* 1998.

Note: Percentages are for nonfarm employment and therefore do not add to 100 percent. Agriculture, private household, and unpaid family work account for the remaining percent.

Tenure with Current Employer (U.S. Workforce)

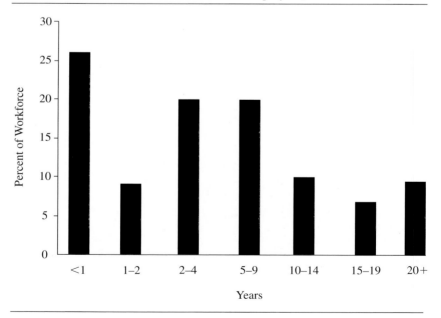

Source: U.S. Bureau of Labor Statistics, "Employee Tenure in the Mid-1990s," 1997.

Number of Jobs in Major Industry Categories (Millions), 1986–2006

	1986	1996	2006
Goods Producing	24.5	24.4	24.5
Mining	0.78	0.57	0.44
Construction	4.8	5.4	5.9
Manufacturing	18.9	18.5	18.1
Service Producing	74.2	94.3	111.9
Transportation and utilities	5.2	6.3	7.1
Wholesale trade	5.8	6.5	7.2
Retail trade	17.9	21.6	23.9
Finance, insurance, and real estate	6.3	6.9	7.7
Services	22.3	33.6	44.9
Government	16.7	19.4	21.1
Agriculture	3.3	3.6	3.6
Private Households	1.2	0.93	0.76
Nonfarm Self-Employed and Unpaid Family	8.1	9.1	10.2

Source: Institute for the Future databases; Franklin, J. C., "Industry Output and Employment Projection to 2006," 1997.

- *Workers need to be self-reliant.* As you enter the workforce, you cannot expect any one company or organization to provide you with job security. Instead, you should seek to develop employment security based on offering skills essential to the entire professional market, rather than to any single employer.
- *The workforce will become more ethnically and gender diverse.* The unique needs of this diverse population will require workers to be flexible to new work styles and organizational structures. The old ***hierarchical*** work model will no longer be as common.

> U.S. consumers spent $3 billion on Internet purchases in 1998, almost $12 billion in 1999, and they are expected to spend more than $41 billion in 2002.

Employment Gains for Women, 1985–1995

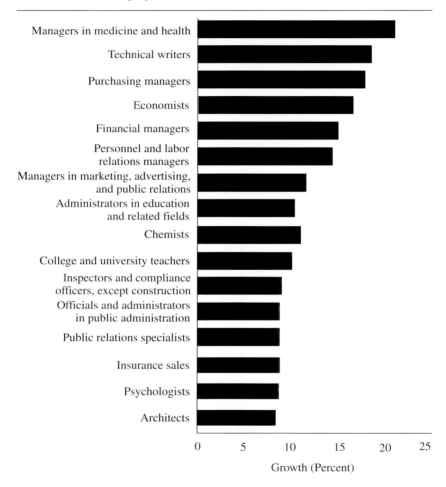

Growth (Percent)

Source: Wooton, B. L., "Gender Differences in Occupational Employment," 1997.

Government Sources for Occupational Forecasts

Occupational Outlook Quarterly
Occupational Outlook Handbook
Occupational Projections and Training
Employment Outlook

Occupational forecasts like these are useful tools for assessing the work world—but like the weather forecast, they are not always right. You should not build your entire career around any such prediction for the future.

- *As the work world grows ever more electronic, global literacy will become increasingly essential.* As more and more media tools become available—such as voice mail, electronic mail, videoconferencing, intranets, and fax—workers will need to have a wide knowledge of the global situation as it pertains to their business. Where a businessperson once only needed to grasp the needs and concerns of his or her personal community, now the business marketplace reaches around the world, requiring a growing sophistication in world awareness.

Today's work world has changed in yet another way as well: our economy today is based more on services than on goods. This means that jobs providing some form of service (whether in the fields of transportation and utilities or in the fields of medicine, education, or retail) will be more plentiful than those jobs where some product is created (like construction or manufacturing). Jobs in retail, government, professional, and personal services are expected to grow faster

Many new jobs in retail and personal services do not require a college education. However, according to the Bureau of Labor Statistics, jobs requiring at least a bachelor's degree pay about 42 percent more than the average job.

than any others; together, they will add 68.8 million jobs to the U.S. job market by 2006.

So how does all this apply to Terrell Washington's situation? Does it mean he should completely abandon his dreams of farming?

As Terrell learns about the current work situation, he certainly needs to take into consideration the realities he will encounter there. Like anyone who is choosing a career, Terrell needs to assess the needs of the real world. But the characteristics of today's work world should not be his only consideration. He also needs to give careful thought to what will make him happiest in the years to come. He needs to consider what role he wants character (including qualities like integrity, respect, justice, citizenship, and courage) to play in his career, and which career will be the best vehicle for that character.

A college degree is one tool you may choose to use for reaching your career goals. In today's work world, however, you cannot expect to "rest on your laurels." No matter how well you did in high school or college, you will need to make lifelong learning a part of your career goals.

Terrell may decide to pursue his dream against the odds; after all, just because there are fewer farming jobs today does not mean there are *no* farming jobs. Terrell may conclude that money is less important to him than the satisfaction of pursuing his grandfather's way of life. Or he may choose to go to college for a degree in horticulture or animal husbandry. Using that degree, he might set up his own Internet business, offering farm products and advice to small gardeners and farmers around the world. His own small farm could be a sideline business that adds pleasure and richness to his life.

Terrell has many options; in fact, over the course of his life he will probably pursue several opportunities, building his skills in a wide variety of ways. The real-life needs of the work world will affect the course of his professional life—but ultimately, he can use those needs to help him shape the career most satisfying to him.

Concentrate on finding your goal,
then concentrate on reaching it.

—Michael Friedman

The Strong Interest Inventory is a paper-and-pencil assessment tool to help you determine what careers interest you most.

4

THE *STRONG INTEREST INVENTORY*

*You will probably find the greatest success
in the careers that interest you most.*

Linda Hernandez didn't know what to expect. Her parents had talked her into making an appointment with her high school guidance counselor, but as she waited nervously in the outer office, Linda almost changed her mind and ducked out the door. The counselor's secretary gave her an encouraging smile, though, and Linda decided to stay. After all, what could it hurt?

Linda knew she needed some help making up her mind about what to do next. She had always wanted to be a gymnast—but in the last year or so, she had faced the sad truth that she just wasn't Olympic material. Of course, she still enjoyed her gymnastics classes, but she knew she needed to make a plan for the years ahead. Her parents had saved money for college, and Linda knew they were expecting her to make up her mind soon about which school she wanted to attend. Linda thought college sounded like fun—but how could she decide which college would be best for her, when she wasn't sure what she wanted to do *after* college?

As she waited nervously for the guidance counselor, she again considered leaving. How could the counselor help her? Mrs. Rankin

According to its publisher, over 30 million people have taken the *Strong Interest Inventory*. It is used by guidance counselors and career counselors in schools, campuses, businesses, and government employment centers.

seemed nice enough, but it wasn't like she really knew Linda. If Linda's own family and friends couldn't help her make up her mind, how could someone who barely knew her?

The counselor's door opened, and Mrs. Rankin stuck her head out. She smiled and said, "Come on in, Linda."

After chatting for a while about Linda's gymnastics, Mrs. Rankin turned the conversation to Linda's reasons for being there. Mrs. Rankin listened as Linda described her problem. "I'm just not sure what I'm interested in doing," Linda finished.

Mrs. Rankin reached onto the shelf behind her and took down a test form. "Here," she said. "Try taking this. We may find it will help us sort out what interests you most—and that will give us some good ideas for

The Strong Interest Inventory can also be administered through computer software or via the Internet.

the direction you should take in college. It's called the *Strong Interest Inventory.*"

The *Strong Interest Inventory* is not a test—so you can't fail it. It's a tool used most often by counselors helping individuals identify their career interests. The paper and pencil inventory (published by Consulting Psychologists Press) usually takes about 35 to 40 minutes. (There is also a shorter, on-line version of the inventory that takes only 15 to 20 minutes.) People over 14 can take the *Strong* to help identify what careers would most interest them. The inventory provides information on 109 different occupations, including those that require vocational or technical training, as well as those requiring a professional education.

> Today's *Strong* is the product of more than 70 years of research. It is continually revised and updated to reflect our ever-changing culture. Researchers consider it to be the most scientific of any career assessment tool.

The *Strong* measures your interests and compares them to those of people already working in a wide range of occupations. If you take the inventory, you will answer 317 questions, where you are asked to rate each item on a three-point scale of "like," "indifferent," and "dislike." The inventory is organized into six vocational personality types:

- **Realistic**
  People who are realistic like jobs that may focus on mechanical, construction, or repair activities. They tend to enjoy working with tools, machines, and equipment. They like action more than thinking.
- **Investigative**
  Investigative people enjoy gather information, and they like analyzing and interpreting data. They often enjoy science, they don't like selling things, and repetitive jobs bore them. Working alone is a better option for these people than team efforts, and they do well pursuing advanced degrees.

- **Artistic**
  People who are artistic need to express themselves creatively. However, they may choose to do this in their spare time rather than as a career. They usually are good with words, and they do well in academic or intellectual environments. Artistic people may express themselves in one of three ways, however: arts, music/dramatics, or writing.
- **Social**
  These people like to work with others. They enjoy sharing responsibilities, caring for others, teaching, helping—and also being the center of attention. Social people tend to solve the problems they encounter by discussing feelings and relationships. They are well-suited to jobs where they lead, direct, or persuade others.
- **Enterprising**
  Individuals who are enterprising talk easily—and they are good at selling and leading. They enjoy working with others, and they often seek positions of leadership and power. Seldom do they enjoy scientific activities or long periods of thought—but they do like taking risks. Competitive activities are fun for them, and they like to work toward (and lead others to) financial and organizational goals.
- **Conventional**
  Conventional people like paying attention to details. They often enjoy math, and they do well in accounting and investment management. They work well in large organizations, and they do their job with accuracy and organization.

Each of these types contains 20 to 33 items on the inventory. No one will ever exactly match a single type of worker, but usually two or three in combination will help you see your general interest patterns.

The *Strong* also has scales that indicate personal styles. These include:

Your guidance counselor can help you understand your Strong Interest Inventory scores.

- work style (prefers to work alone vs. prefers working with people);
- learning style (prefers practical, hands-on learning environment vs. academic learning environment);
- leadership style (prefers to lead by example vs. prefers taking charge and motivating others);
- propensity for adventure/risk-taking (prefers to play it safe vs. prefers adventure and risk-taking).

The inventory only measures *interests,* not *skills.* So it can't predict whether you have the aptitude to succeed in a particular occupational field. It is not meant to tell you what you "should do"; it can only point the way toward the first step of exploring what interests you most.

After you take the *Strong,* if you used the paper-and-pencil ver-

> To find out what one is fitted to do, and to secure an opportunity to do it, is the key to happiness.
> —John Dewey

The *Strong Interest Inventory* contains these basic interest scales:

- agriculture (working outdoors)
- nature (appreciating nature)
- military activities (working in structured settings)
- athletics (playing or watching sports)
- mechanical activities (working with tools and equipment)
- science (conducting scientific research)
- mathematics (working with numbers or statistics)
- medical science (working in medicine or biology)
- music/dramatics (performing or enjoying music/drama)
- art (appreciating or creating art)
- applied arts (producing or enjoying visual art)
- writing (reading or writing)
- culinary arts (cooking or entertaining)
- teaching (instructing young people)
- social service (helping people)
- medical service (helping people in a medical setting)
- religious activities (participating in spiritual activities)
- public speaking (persuading or influencing people)
- law/politics (discussing law and public policies)
- merchandising (selling retail or wholesale products)
- sales (selling to potential customers)
- organizational management (managing or supervising others)
- data management (analyzing data for decision making)
- computer activities (working with computers)
- office services (performing clerical and office tasks)

Adapted from the *Strong Interest Inventory* Profile, Stanford, Calif.: Stanford University Press, 1994.

sion, your counselor will not have the results for about three weeks after he or she mails it to the inventory's publisher. However, if you take a software or on-line version of the inventory, you can get immediate scores.

If, like Linda, you're confused about which direction to head after high school, the *Strong Interest Inventory* can help you understand yourself better, so that you get moving toward your future career life. The inventory may suggest to you new occupational fields you've never considered—or it may confirm for you that a field you've already chosen is a good "fit." It may also help you see the types of people you would enjoy working with as coworkers or clients.

If you take this inventory, remember: there are no right or wrong answers. Try to answer as honestly as possible; don't try to guess what the counselor (or your parents—or anyone else) wants you to put down on the paper. Take your time . . . and don't expect a magic answer. The *Strong* is not a well-researched fortune cookie.

It *is* a powerful tool that can help you explore career options. The more information you have about yourself and the world of work, the better equipped you will be for making the important decisions that lie ahead. If you find you still need more help making up your mind, there are other career tools you can use.

Destiny is not a matter of chance, it is a matter of choice; it is not a thing to be waited for, it is a thing to be achieved.

—William Jennings Bryan

Before you apply for any job, it's a good idea to know where your skills and interests lie.

5

THE *CAMPBELL INTEREST AND SKILL SURVEY*

Finding the areas where you feel both interested and self-confident is one step toward choosing a career.

Howie Chen was pretty sure he knew what he wanted to do: he wanted to be an architect. As a boy he had loved designing and building elaborate constructions out of his building toys—and he figured architecture was as close as he could get to that childhood pleasure.

His parents and teachers, however, wondered if architecture was the right career for him. He had never done particularly well in math; in fact, he had never gotten high grades in any subject except gym. Everyone except Howie seemed certain he would do better in a more active, less academic career.

Howie was pretty certain he could do well at anything that really interested him—he had just never been particularly interested in his schoolwork. But his parents and teachers could be right about him. Maybe he just wasn't cut out to be an architect. Maybe there was some other career out there that would be better suited to his skills and interests.

To help him feel clearer about his plan for the future, his school guidance counselor encouraged him to take the *Campbell Interest and*

The Campbell Interest and Skill Survey can be taken with paper and pencil—or with computer software or on-line.

Skill Survey (*CISS*), a tool designed to help individuals make decisions about their careers. The survey relates interests and skills to the real-life work world.

The *CISS* can be taken as a paper-and-pencil survey, with computer software, or on-line. It takes about 35 to 45 minutes, and consists of 200 interest items and 120 skill items. You will be asked to rate your level of interest according to a six-point scale (ranging from "strongly like" to "strongly dislike"), and you will rate your skills along a six-point scale as well (from "expert: widely recognized as excellent in this area" to "none: have no skill in this area").

The survey can't measure your actual skills. But it can indicate your level of self-confidence in a specific skill. It also allows you to consider the things that interest you most in comparison to your degree

The *Campbell Interest and Skill Survey* is designed specifically for students who are college bound or for individuals considering careers that require college degrees.

of self-confidence in those areas. These patterns of interest and skills can then provide you with suggestions for career possibilities where you may find both satisfaction and success. You will probably find you have some interests and skills in all seven of the *CISS* groups. Hopefully, however, you will see clusters of both interests and skills in one or more groups. The *CISS* will give you four possible options:

> The fun of being alive is realizing you have a talent and you can use it every day so it grows stronger.
> —Lou Centlivre

The *Campbell Interest and Skill Survey* is organized around seven factors, referred to as orientations:

1. influencing (leadership)
2. organizing (management and financial services)
3. helping (teachers, counselors, healers)
4. creating (music/drama, art, writing)
5. analyzing (science, math, computer activities)
6. producing (mechanical, construction, and farming activities)
7. adventuring (military, police, and athletic activities)

- **Pursue (high interest–high skill)**
  This is an area where you would feel both interested and confident. You would be likely to experience both satisfaction and success, so this is an area you should definitely consider pursuing.
- **Develop (high interest–lower skill)**
  This pattern indicates an area where you have potential to grow. You might want to consider it as a hobby or leisure activity—or if you are interested and motivated enough, you might want to consider gaining additional education or training to build your confidence level.
- **Explore (lower interest–high skill)**
  When you see this pattern in a particular area, you may want to consider applying the particular skill you possess to a new field that might interest you more. For instance, although you may

The *CISS* contains these basic interest and skill scales:

- leadership (acquire resources, inspire others to do their best)
- law/politics (debate and negotiate)
- public speaking (give interviews, deliver speeches, conduct training)
- sales (persuade others to buy goods or services)
- advertising/marketing (create marketing strategies, design advertising campaigns)
- supervision (manage other workers, plan budgets, schedule work)
- financial services (provide advice on investments and economics)
- office practices (perform secretarial tasks; handle schedules, supplies, and files)
- adult development (teach new skills to adults)
- counseling (advising and supporting people)
- child development (teach, tell stories, play with children)
- religious activities (conduct religious programs)
- medical practice (provide medical care or first aid)
- art/design (draw, design, create works of art)
- performing arts (play music, act, sing, dance, or direct plays)
- writing (research, write, edit)
- international activities (travel, speak foreign languages)
- fashion (design clothing, buy and sell clothes or jewelry)

- culinary arts (cook, manage a restaurant)
- mathematics (write computer programs, analyze data, teach mathematics)
- science (research, work with scientific concepts and equipment)
- mechanical crafts (work with cars, machines, and electrical systems)
- woodworking (carpentry, furniture building)
- farming/forestry (raise crops, manage timbers, care for livestock)
- plants/gardens (design and care for gardens)
- animal care (care for pets, raise and train animals)
- athletics/physical fitness (exercise, coach, compete)
- military/law enforcement (use military strategies in dangerous situations)
- risk/adventure (high-risk, exciting, physically strenuous activities)

Adapted from Jeffrey P. Prince and Lisa J. Heiser, *Essentials of Career Interest and Assessment* (New York: John Wiley & Sons, 2000), pp. 90–91.

do very well in mathematics, you are bored with jobs that focus on statistics or computer analysis. If you also enjoy teaching, you might instead consider becoming a high school math teacher.

- **Avoid (low interest–low skill)**
  When you see this pattern it indicates you have neither interest nor skills in this particular field. Unless you have some other reason for pursuing a career in this field (for instance, if tradition demands you take over a family business), you shouldn't even bother to consider a career in this area. If you do have some compelling reason for pursuing a career in this field, be aware you will need to find ways to add both interest and skills to your professional life.

One limitation of the *CISS* is that it only lists 60 possible occupations. Obviously, there are thousands of other jobs in the world—so don't consider the results from this survey to be the final list of your career options. Instead, you may want to brainstorm as many jobs as possible that could be related to the occupations listed in the results of your *CISS*.

You may think your own assessments of your skills can't be trusted. However, research reported in the *CISS* manual indicates that individuals usually recognize their own skills accurately.

Like the *Strong Interest Inventory*, the *CISS* is not a test you can pass or fail. You should answer the questions carefully but quickly. Don't spend too much time thinking about a particular item, second-guessing yourself; go with your initial "gut" feeling.

The *CISS* is intended to supply you with a full-range assessment of life interests and skills. This means it is not meant to only point you toward a specific career. Because the survey indicates you have a high level of interest and self-confidence in gardening, for instance, may not mean you need to pursue gardening as your life career. That would certainly be one option you might consider; but you might decide instead to make gardening a lifelong hobby.

After Howie finished taking the survey, he discovered his results indicated that architecture might be a good career for him after all. Of course, the *CISS* couldn't guarantee his success in this field—but the survey results gave him the courage to stick to his guns and pursue his

When using the *CISS*, high school students should "use a grain of salt" whenever they see an "Avoid" tag on some career area. You may lack confidence and interest in this field simply because you can't really assess either your interest or your skills; you may lack the experience or exposure to this area you would need to judge accurately. Consider moving "Avoid" categories into the "Explore" or "Develop" categories.

childhood dream. The counselor encouraged him to share the results with his parents, as a communication tool.

Howie left the guidance office feeling less confused. He knew if he needed further direction in the weeks ahead, the counselor had other tools as well he could use to fine-tune his career plan for the future.

We can do whatever we wish to do provided our wish is strong enough. . . . What do you most want to do? That's what I keep asking myself, in the face of difficulties.

—Katherine Mansfield

Before you check the want ads for a job after graduation, take time to use some of the assessment tools that can help you pick the jobs best suited for you.

6

THE *SELF-DIRECTED SEARCH*

*Use whatever tools you can find to help
you choose what's right for you.*

Sherry Zarsinki didn't feel like talking to one more adult about her career options. She knew she needed more information before she could make any decisions about the future—but when she talked to adults, she always seemed to end up more confused than she had been before. Everything was always so clear and simple for her parents, teachers, and the guidance counselor; as Sherry listened to them, she would find herself agreeing with them, simply because they were so certain. She respected their advice—but she wanted to do what was right for *her,* not what the adults in her life thought she should do. Standing up for herself was hard, though . . . especially when she was so unsure about what she wanted.

Mr. Hawkins, the guidance counselor, seemed to sense how she was feeling. He suggested she should do some career assessment on her own for a while. He gave her a survey to take, the *Self-Directed Search,* that she could understand by herself, without waiting for him to tell her what it meant. Sherry liked the feeling of being in control. Glad that Mr. Hawkins had understood what she needed, she sat down in a quiet corner of the guidance office and began to take the test.

The *Self-Directed Search (SDS)* is one of the most simple of all career assessments. It is a self-administered, self-scored, and self-

> Each of us has some unique
> capability waiting for realization.
> . . . Each of us can bring to
> fruition these innate abilities.
> —George H. Bender

interpreted interest inventory that's designed to help you find jobs that best suit your interests and skills. The booklet contains 228 items that include four scales (Activities, Competencies, Occupations, and Self-Estimates). It also has an Occupational Daydream section that measures the six types of workers:

- realistic
- investigative
- artistic
- social
- enterprising
- conventional

The Self-Directed Search allows you to find jobs that best match your interests—all by yourself, without help from a counselor or teacher.

(If these categories are starting to sound familiar, that's because both Strong and Campbell borrowed ideas from John Holland, the author of the *SDS*.) The inventory takes from 30 to 50 minutes, and it is available as a paper and pencil test, as software, and on the Internet.

Realistic Personality Type

If you score high in this area, then you would probably enjoy being an automobile mechanic, an aircraft controller, a surveyor, a farmer, or an electrician. You may have a great deal of mechanical ability but lack some social skills. These adjectives might apply to you:

conforming	materialistic
frank	persistent
genuine	practical
hardheaded	thrifty
inflexible	self-effacing

Investigative Personality Type

According to the *SDS,* this type of person likes jobs such as these: biologist, chemist, physicist, anthropologist, geologist, and medical technologist. If you are this type of person, you may have plenty of mathematical and scientific ability and yet lack leadership skills. These adjectives may describe you:

analytical	pessimistic
cautious	precise
critical	rational
complex	reserved
curious	retiring
independent	unassuming
intellectual	unpopular
introspective	

Famous Examples of the *SDS* Personality Types

<u>Realistic</u>	<u>Investigative</u>	<u>Artistic</u>
Thomas Edison	Madame Curie	T.S. Eliot
Admiral Byrd	Charles Darwin	Pablo Picasso
<u>Social</u>	<u>Enterprising</u>	<u>Conventional</u>
Jane Addams	Henry Ford	John D. Rockefeller
Albert Schweitzer	Andrew Carnegie	Bernard Baruch

Taken from information provided by the *SDS* Technical Manual by John L. Holland (Odessa, Fla.: Psychological Assessment Resources, 1994).

The Artistic Type of Personality

If your *SDS* score indicates you have this personality, you might enjoy being a composer, musician, stage director, writer, interior decorator, or actor/actress. You have artistic abilities—but you may lack clerical skills. You can be described as:

complicated	independent
disorderly	introspective
emotional	intuitive
expressive	nonconforming
idealistic	open
imaginative	original
impractical	sensitive
impulsive	

The Social Type of Personality

If you have this type of personality, then you will most likely enjoy jobs where you interact with people, like being a teacher, religious worker, counselor, clinical psychologist, psychiatric caseworker, or speech therapist. You are socially adept—but you may lack mechanical and scientific ability. These adjectives may apply to you:

cooperative	patient
empathic	persuasive
friendly	responsible
generous	sociable
helpful	tactful
idealistic	understanding
kind	warm

Each graduate is a unique package of talents, abilities, and interests. In the years ahead, take time to determine the contents of your "package."

The Enterprising Type of Personality

According to the *SDS,* people with this personality type make good salespeople, managers, business executives, television producers, sports promoters, and buyers. If you fall into this category, you may have a great deal of leadership and speaking ability, while you are likely to lack scientific ability. You can be described as:

acquisitive	exhibitionistic
adventurous	extroverted
agreeable	flirtatious
ambitious	optimistic
domineering	self-confident
energetic	sociable
excitement-seeking	talkative

The Conventional Type of Personality

If the characteristics of this personality type match yours, you would probably enjoy being a bookkeeper, stenographer, financial advisor, banker, or tax expert. You may have clerical and arithmetic skill but lack any artistic ability. You may also find that these adjectives apply to you:

careful	obedient
conforming	orderly
conscientious	persistent
defensive	practical
efficient	prudish
inflexible	thrifty
inhibited	unimaginative
methodical	

As you can see, each personality type has its own package of strengths and weaknesses. Choosing the right career for you entails

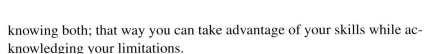

knowing both; that way you can take advantage of your skills while acknowledging your limitations.

If you don't score high in at least one personality type, don't be discouraged. You may simply not have enough information yet—or you may have been in the wrong mood to focus on the survey. Gather more information, give yourself some time, and then try taking the survey again.

When Sherry Zarsinski finished the survey, she felt like she understood herself better than she had before. She had a few questions she wanted to ask the guidance counselor about the results—but for now, she wanted to take some time to just mull over everything she had learned.

"When you get home," Mr. Hawkins suggested, "here's some career sites you can check out on the Internet." He handed her a sheet of paper with a list of web sites. "And if you come back tomorrow, I have some career computer programs you might want to take a look at."

Sherry had a lot to think about. And she was eager to discover what else she could learn.

The same person cannot be skilled in everything; each has his special excellence.

—Euripides

The Internet and computer software can be good sources for career assessment.

7

Computer and Internet Career Guidance

*The world is full of information on which to
build your choices for the future.*

ike Terry Zarsinski, Alec Jackson wanted to check out career options on his own. Since he was only a sophomore in high school, he
figured he had plenty of time to make up his mind. He just wanted to
start getting some ideas, and he was more comfortable sitting in front of
a computer than he was with a pencil in his hand. Getting some career
guidance from computer programs and the Internet seemed like a good
way to begin.

His guidance counselor let him sit down at the computer and
showed him what was available. There was so much material, Alec
knew he would have to come back another time to get through
everything.

DISCOVER

This computer program offers a multimedia experience, complete
with videos, slides, graphics, and audio screen directions. It has both
Windows and Macintosh versions, and it is organized into four
"halls":

1. Learn about Self and Career
2. Choose Occupations
3. Plan My Education
4. Plan for Work

In Hall 1, the program allows users to complete inventories that will allow them to better understand their interests, abilities, and work values. DISCOVER immediately scores and interprets these results by plotting them on the "World-of-Work Map." As users move on to Hall 2, they can view narrated videos of the jobs they have identified as most suited to themselves. They can also search extensive databases related to their field of interest. Moving on to Hall 3, the

> The road to happiness lies in two simple principles: find what interests you and that you can do well, and put your whole soul into it—every bit of energy and ambition and natural ability you have.
> —John D. Rockefeller III

On-line career inventories allow you to gain information in the relaxed environment of your own home.

Other Career Assessment Web Sites

Take Hold of Your Future
www.ncasi.com/thoyf

Quintessential Careers
www.quintcareers.com/teens.html

Kruder® Career Planning System
www.kruder.com

The Self-Directed Search
www.self-directed-search.com

Self-Assessment Center at Monster.com
tools.monster.com

users identify college majors, find appropriate schools, and determine sources of financial aid. At last, in Hall 4, users learn about apprenticeships and internship opportunities. The program instructs them how to conduct a job search and prepare for interviewing. DISCOVER also provides hyperlinks to related web sites, such as colleges and job banks.

SIGI PLUS

This program, one of the most commonly used computerized career guidance systems, is another self-directed, ***interactive*** system that provides both information and guidance to individuals exploring the field of careers. It offers first an in-depth self-assessment that allows users to see more clearly their work values, their interests, and their skills. These results are then used to identify potential occupations—and these in turn can be searched for information on 27 different dimensions, including work activities, educational requirements, and beginning, average, and top earnings. SIGI PLUS also offers up-to-date information on colleges and graduate schools and practical advice on financial aid, time management, and the potential rewards and chances of succeeding in various career options. Perhaps most important, the program helps users create short-range goals for the future, as well as the practical action steps needed to achieve those goals.

Alec Jackson enjoyed exploring career options in an individualized electronic environment. He liked the sense of independence he felt as got to know himself and the work world a little better. Whenever he was ready, he knew he could talk with a guidance or career counselor, a professional who could offer him still more tools for making up his mind about his career.

The aim of self-development is to realize one's nature perfectly.

—Oscar Wilde

~~75~~ ~~75~~ 80
/100

True or False

1. F The Works Spreadsheet tool can crea
spreadsheet. *Chart Tool*

2. T To start the Works Spreadsheet tool, choo
Works for Windows group window in Prog

3. T The intersection of a column and a row is

4. F Columns are identified by numbers and rows a
alphabet.

5. T A highlighted cell is identified by a heavy border

6. T The Cancel box and the Enter box are displayed in

7. T Pressing the Enter key accomplishes the same task as
box when entering data into a cell.

8. T When you enter text, the text is placed in the highlighted ce
in the cell.

9. F To cancel an entry before entering it into a cell, press the ESC k
the Enter box.

10. F When you press the Right Arrow key after typing data in a cell, Works
the data in the cell to the right of the highlighted cell.

11. T Numeric data can be summed using the Autosum button on the Toolba

12. F To format a number with a dollar sign, comma and decimal point, you must
click the Currency button on the Toolbar prior to typing the numeric value.

13. T When you use the Autosum button to add numbers, Works highlights what
it considers your choice of the group of cells to sum by first looking at the
range of numbers above the highlighted cell and then to the right of the
highlighted cell.

14. T When you copy cell references in a formula, Works automatically adjusts the
cell references for each new position of the formula.

*If paper-and-pencil tests make you anxious, you may find a card sort to be
the right career assessment tool for you.*

8

CARD SORTS

Understanding yourself is one of the
first steps toward understanding
the world of work.

Doreen Williams hated writing. And she hated sitting in front of the computer. Maybe that's why she had never liked school much. All those little letters in neat little rows just made her head hurt. She loved to paint and draw, and she was good at sports—but academics had just never been her thing.

So as Doreen thought about the years after high school, she sometimes felt scared. She knew most people needed some sort of college education or training to get good paying jobs—but the thought of going back to school again after her senior year of high school filled her with dismay.

When her guidance counselor asked to meet with her, Doreen was reluctant. For the past few months, Doreen had been operating under the assumption that if she could just put off thinking about the future, it would somehow take care of itself. Why should she ruin the fun she was having right now by worrying about the years ahead?

Her guidance counselor, however, apparently understood Doreen better than she expected. Instead of asking Doreen to complete a paper and pencil test or sitting her down in front of a computer, he got out a set of cards. Doreen listened as he explained that the cards would give her visual cues to which she could respond. As she sorted through the pictures on the cards, she would also be sorting out her work values and interests.

With a sigh of relief, Doreen sat back in her chair. This was a task she could handle.

> What is the recipe for successful achievement? To my mind there are just four essential ingredients:
>
> Choose a career you love. . . .
> Give it the best there is in you. . . .
> Seize your opportunities. . . .
> And be a member of the team.
>
> —Benjamin F. Fairless

Talent Sort 2000

The 52 cards in this career assessment tool each contain a cartoon that illustrates a particular activity. Beneath the cartoon on each card is a single word that corresponds to the picture (for example, building, developing, calculating, etc.). The cards have a bright contemporary look, and users can go through them in as little as ten minutes. The cards

Sometimes it's more productive—and more fun—to share the results of your career assessments in a group.

Possible Jobs (within the Finance Industry) for Each Talent Sort 2000 Category

PEOPLE
chief financial officer
stockbroker
mortgage banker
personal banker
financial planner
receptionist
mortgage broker

DATA
comptroller
real estate appraiser
tax analyst
insurance underwriter
accountant
loan officer
bookkeeper

THINGS
engraver
locksmith
general office clerk
security systems specialist
computer service technician
microfilm operator
data base technician

IDEAS
economist
policy analyst
product developer
investment banker
advertiser
computer systems analyst
copyright specialist

Adapted from Talent Sort 2000 manual, Master Works (Annandale, Virginia: 1998).

are divided into four categories—data, ideas, people, and things—to help users determine which area would suit them best from a career perspective.

To use the cards, users shuffle them and then deal them face up into four rows of 13 cards each. Users then select the 10 cards that best represent their interests. After turning over the selected cards, users count how many they have in each "suit" (blue = data, red = ideas, yellow = people, and green = things). Users then view the Occupations Card for that suit to select possible occupations to explore further. There are six Occupational Cards, one each for data, ideas, people, and things, and then two more that suggest occupations based on people and things combined. Each Occupational Card suggests 21 to 25 occupations users can consider.

This card sort can be done alone, with a counselor, or even with a group of friends. If you do this card sort alone, it's a good idea to get feedback from someone else you trust. For instance, you and a group of friends might want to assess each other. Do your friends see you as being more interested in data, ideas, people, or things—or a combination of two or more? You and your friends might want to brainstorm other occupations you might enjoy in your category, other than the ones listed on the cards.

ValueSearch

This card sort tool can help you clarify your work values. In other words, you can use this technique to determine what is really most important to you as you enter the world of work.

The 60 cards each contain a single word that relates to a value. Here are some examples:

accomplishment	recognition
balance	adventure
challenge	artistic expression
duty	competition
family	creativity
fun	faith
health	friendship
high earnings	independence
leadership	learning
love	status
nature	team work

Users begin using the cards by sorting them into four categories: always valued, often valued, sometimes valued, and never valued. Users can also add words not included on the cards. Then users pick their top ten values, and discuss (or write) what those words mean to them.

These values will usually demonstrate a cluster in one of eight categories:

1. Universality (understanding, appreciation, tolerance, and protection of all people and nature).
2. Benevolence (concern for the welfare of those people with whom one is in close contact).
3. Tradition (respect for and commitment to the customs and ideas of one's religion or culture).
4. Security (desire for safety and stability in relationships and society).
5. Power (attainment of social status, prestige, influence, or authority of people and resources).
6. Achievement (desire for personal success or accomplishment).
7. Excitement (enjoyment of pleasure, sensuous gratification, and variety).
8. Self-direction (appreciation of opportunities for independent thought and action, choice, and exploration).

Once you are more aware of your values, you will probably find that career or guidance counselors can help you connect your values to practical career options. These professionals can also help you sort through conflicts in your values—for example when the cards you pick as your ten most important values are split between "Benevolence" and "Power." You may discover you can meet your need for a particular value through your work life while you satisfy another value in your private life. If the conflict is too deep, however, that's merely a sign that before you go any further in the process of selecting a career, you need to spend some time thinking through what you truly value most in life.

Other Card Sorts

Motivated Skills Card Sort
Occupational Interest Card Sort
Occ-U-Sort
Slaney Vocational Card Sort
Vocational Exploration and
Insight Kit

As Doreen Williams used various card sort tools, she gained information about herself and the world of work. She talked more with her guidance counselor and her friends, and as a result, she began to sort that information into the knowledge she needed to move ahead into her future. For instance, as she matched her interests and values to the job world, she realized that some vocational training programs interested her, as well as two-year college programs in commercial art.

Doreen still had a long way to go before she achieved the wisdom she needed to map her future life. But she felt good she had taken the first steps on her career journey.

The very first step towards success in any occupation is to become interested in it.

—Sir William Osler

Choosing a career may seem like a gamble, with no guarantees that you'll "hit the jackpot."

9

THE LIMITATIONS OF
CAREER ASSESSMENTS

*Even the best forecasts for the
future are sometimes wrong.*

Jake Martinez was frustrated. He had done everything he was sup-
posed to do as he chose a career for himself. When his guidance
counselor advised that he use various career assessment tools, he had
happily complied. One by one, he had worked his way through all
the surveys, tests, and activities. He had listened carefully as his
guidance counselor explained that he was ideally suited for a career
as a lawyer. His high school grades were high enough to get him into
a good pre-law program; later, he did so well as an undergraduate
that he had gotten into one of the top Ivy League law schools. Of
course he had had to work hard, but even the bar exam had come rel-
atively easy to him. His family, his friends, and Jake himself had all
felt certain he was on his way to the wealth and prestige of a career
in law.

So what had gone wrong? Two years after he passed his bar
exam, he was stuck in a small-town law office, checking deeds. He
was bored with his work—and his brother who had gone into
plumbing was making more money than he was. What was the point

of all those career assessments? They had landed him in a job he hated.

No career assessment technique, no matter how scientific and well researched, can provide you with a failsafe formula for occupational happiness. For several reasons, they cannot claim to accurately predict your future.

First of all, no matter how many facts you gather, you can't add them all up and reach a definite answer. The "whole" (your ideal lifelong career) cannot be predicted from the sum of the "parts" (your current interests, skills, and values related to the current real-life work world). There will always be some factors you can't control that may change the picture that lies ahead in the future.

Another reason why career assessments sometimes seem to fail is because you may place too much trust in them. No counselor or assessment tool has the authority to tell you who you are or what you should do. Howard Figler, author of *The Career Counselor's Handbook*, recommends that rather than relying on any score or test prediction, you should place more trust in your answers to these questions:

- What do I feel instinctively that I ought to do with my life?
- Which careers keep coming back to my mind?
- Which careers am I most curious about?
- If I could have a magic wand and try any career I wanted for a year, which would it be?

When young people begin shaping their careers, they sometimes forget that choosing an occupation is likely to be a lifelong process. As a young adult, you are still changing and growing. What interests you a great deal at 17 may no longer be as fascinating when you are 27. By the same token, that aptitude you lack as a senior in high school may no longer look so daunting as you mature; you may find that with diligence and self-discipline you are able to master skills you never suspected you could. Figler recommends that this question also be a part of any career assessment process: *How do I want to be*

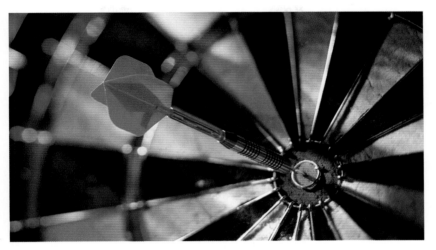

Picking a career is not like playing darts—you don't have to hit the center on your first try. Instead, you may need time to find the career option that's best for you—or what works for you at one stage in your life may not work as well at other stages.

different tomorrow so that my career goals will be more likely to come true?

Like Jake, you may try a career and find you hate it. But be sure not to give up too soon. It may be that Jake simply needs to find a job in another law office. Or he may need to be patient as he gains the experience and knowledge he needs to merit a more exciting law job.

By the same token, you may long to pursue a career everyone else tells you will never work. Your family, friends, teachers, and guidance counselor may all insist you'd be far more suited for another line of work. But something deep inside keeps nudging you in that same "foolish" direction. When that happens, you should gather all the information and insight you can, from as many sources as you can. Carefully consider the facts: who you are (what interests you, what you're good at, what you value) and what the work world is like. See if there's a way you can make your dream work. Sometimes, taking a risk is worth it in the end. When we shoot for the stars, we may not hit them

Predictions That Flopped

There is no reason for any individual to have a computer in their home.
  —Kenneth Olsen, president and founder of Digital Equipment Corporation, in 1977

Airplanes are interesting toys but of no military value.
  —Marshal Ferdinand Foch, French military strategist, in 1911

[Human beings will never reach the moon] regardless of all future scientific advances.
  —Lee DeForest, inventor of the audion tube, in 1967

[Television] won't be able to hold on to any market it captures after the first six months. People will soon get tired of staring at a plywood box every night.
  —Darryl F. Zanuck, head of 20th Century Fox, in 1946

This "telephone" has too many shortcomings to be seriously considered as a means of communication. The device is inherently of no value to us.
  —Western Union memo, in 1876

Everything that can be invented has been invented.
  —Charles H. Duell, U.S. Commissioner of Patents, in 1899

on the first try . . . but who knows what will happen if we just keep trying?

Bottom line: It's all up to you. Only you can decide what's best for your life.

Always bear in mind that your own resolution to success is more important than any other one thing.

—Abraham Lincoln

If you think of your career as a race, then all you will care about is "getting ahead"—but if you see your career as a vehicle for doing good in the world, then character issues will be important to you.

10

A CHOICE TO DO GOOD

*Take control of your life: choose
to make a difference.*

*W*ould *you tell me please which way I ought to walk from here?"*
    "That depends a great deal on where you want to get to," said the
Cat.
    "I don't much care where—" said Alice.
    "Then it doesn't matter which way you walk," said the Cat.
    As this paragraph from Lewis Carroll's *The Adventures of Alice in
Wonderland* illustrates, choosing a direction for your life is important.
If you just wander around, with no real goal in mind, you're not likely
to end up much of anywhere.
    Sometimes, though, we act as though we have no choices in life.
We just react to whatever comes along . . . and we get frustrated and angry when what comes along isn't all we might like. Ultimately, we feel
helpless to become who we want to be. We are powerless, swept along
by the tides of chance.
    But you don't have to be a ***reactive*** person; instead, you can choose
to be ***proactive.*** You can take control of your own life. Of course proactive people can't control everything that happens to them. But they can
control what they do about life's events. They make their choices based
on the core character values we mentioned in chapter 2: honesty and
trustworthiness, respect and compassion, justice and fairness, responsi-

> A life that hasn't a definite plan is likely to become driftwood.
> —David Sarnoff

> If you don't know where you are going, how can you expect to get there?
> —Basil S. Walsh

bility, courage, self-discipline and diligence, and citizenship. They choose to set goals for their life—and they use life's events, no matter how difficult, as steppingstones toward the future.

According to John Bytheway, author of *What I Wish I'd Known in High School,* reactive people have handed the remote control for their lives to someone or something else. In effect, they're saying, "Here, change my emotions, my circumstance, my life however you want." Then they're stuck watching whatever

Reactive Language

I'll try.
There's nothing I can do about it.
That's just the way I am.
I can't.
I have to.
You ruined my day.

Proactive Language

I'll do it.
Let's look at all our options.
I can do better than that if you'll give me the chance.
I can find a way.
I choose to.
I'm not going to let your actions or bad mood rub off on me.

Adapted from Sean Covey, *The 7 Habits of Highly Effective Teens* (New York: Simon & Schuster, 1998), p. 51.

Reactive vs. Proactive People

- Reactive people think of themselves as victims. Proactive people believe they have power to make choices.
- Reactive people are easily offended. Proactive people aren't.
- Reactive people blame others. Proactive people take responsibility for their choices.
- Reactive people get angry and then say and do things they later regret. Proactive people think before they act.
- Reactive people whine and complain. Proactive people bounce back when something bad happens.
- Reactive people wait for things to happen to them. Proactive people find a way to make things happen.
- Reactive people change only when they have to. Proactive people focus on things they can change and don't worry about things they can't.

Adapted from Sean Covey, *The 7 Habits of Highly Effective Teens* (New York: Simon & Schuster, 1998), pp. 52-53.

"show" is picked by whoever's holding the remote. Proactive people, however, hold the remote control in their own hands. They are free to choose whatever "channel" they want.

If you decide to be a proactive person, your career will be one of the biggest choices you'll ever make. We usually think of the word "career" as meaning "a job or occupation." The original Latin and French root words meant "a cart" or "a racecourse." If you think of your career as a cart, then it is something that carries your interior skills, personality, and character to the outside world around you. According to this definition, making a positive difference may be what's most important to you as you determine the right career for you. If, however,

> Whether I fail or succeed shall be no one's doing but my own. I am the force.
> —Elaine Maxwell

One tool that will help you form goals and work toward them is a personal mission statement. Companies have mission statements that summarize what they are all about— and now more and more, people are encouraged to do the same. By putting your goals and values into writing, you become clearer about what is really most important to you— and if you keep your mission statement somewhere you will see it often, it will remind you to stay on track.

> If a man is called to be a streetsweeper, he should sweep streets even as Michelangelo painted, or Beethoven composed music, or Shakespeare wrote poetry. He should sweep streets so well that all the hosts in heaven and earth will pause to say, here lived a great streetsweeper who did his job well.
> —Martin Luther King, Jr.

you think of your career as a racetrack, then you may be more focused on goals and winning; your ambition may be the most important factor for determining your career.

What about you? Do you see career as a cart—or a racecourse? The work you do in life can be your own personal opportunity to do good in the world—or it can be simply a way for you to focus on yourself, gaining power, money, and possessions. The choice is up to you.

If one advances confidently in the direction of his dreams, and endeavors to live the life which he has imagined, he will meet with success unexpected. . . .

—Henry David Thoreau

FURTHER READING

Borgen, F. and J. Grutter. *Where Do I Go Next? Using Your Strong Results to Manage Your Career.* Palo Alto, Calif.: Consulting Psychologists Press, 1995.

Covey, Sean. *The 7 Habits of Highly Effective Teens.* New York: Simon & Schuster, 1998.

Hall, D. T., editor. *The Career Is Dead, Long Live the Career.* San Francisco: Jossey-Bass, 1996.

Josephson, Michael S. and Wes Hanson, editors. *The Power of Character.* San Francisco: Jossey-Bass, 1998.

Kidder, Rushworth M. *How Good People Make Tough Choices.* New York: Simon & Schuster, 1995.

Kummerow, Jean M., editor. *New Directions in Career Planning and the Workplace.* Palo Alto, Calif.: Davies-Black, 2000.

McGraw, Jay. *Life Strategies for Teens.* New York: Simon & Schuster, 2000.

FOR MORE INFORMATION

America's Career InfoNet
www.acinet.org/acinet

America's Job Bank
www.ajb.dni.us

Campbell Interest and Skill Survey
National Computer Systems
    Assessments
P.O. Box 1416
Minneapolis, Minnesota 55440
612-939-5000
www.usnews.com/usnews/edu/career
    s/ccciss.htm

Center for the 4th and 5th Rs
www.cortland.edu/c4n5rs

Character Education Network
www.charactered.net

DISCOVER
www.act.org/discover/

Josephson Institute of Ethics
www.josephsoninstitute.org

The *Self-Directed Search*
Pychological Assessment Resources
P.O. Box 998
Odessa, Florida 33556
www.self-directed-search.com

The *Strong Interest Inventory*
Consulting Psychologists Press
3803 East Bayshore Road
P.O. Box 10096
Palo Alto, California 94303
800-624-1765
www.cpp-db.com/products/strong

Talent Sort 2000
Mastery Works
6724 Old McLean Village Drive,
    Suite 200
McLean, Virginia 22101
800-691-8379
www.masteryworks.com

GLOSSARY

Assessment   A determination of importance, value, and other characteristics.

Cyclical   Occurring again and again in a repeating pattern.

Entry requirements   What you need to enter a job at the bottom level.

Genetic   Having to do with the chromosomes passed from parents to their offspring, which carry the code determining the characteristics of each organism.

Holistic   Concerned with the complete system rather than just a piece of it.

Interactive   Involving two-way communication.

Linear career growth   Professional progress along a straight line (rather than cycles).

Paternalism   A system where an authority figure undertakes to supply all the needs and control the behavior of those under him.

Proactive   Acting in a take-charge way that assumes responsibility for the future.

Reactive   Acting in response to an emotion or circumstances.

Tenure   A status of security granted in some positions after a specific amount of time spent working in that position.

Trade journal   A publication put out by a particular occupation.

INDEX

BIOGRAPHIES

Ellyn Sanna has authored more than 50 books, including adult nonfiction, novels, young adult biographies, and gift books. She also works as a freelance editor and helps care for three children, a cat, a rabbit, a one-eyed hamster, two turtles, and a hermit crab.

Cheryl Gholar is a Community and Economic Development Educator with the University of Illinois Extension. She has a Ph.D. in Educational Leadership and Policy Studies from Loyola University, and she has more than 20 years of experience with the Chicago Public Schools as a teacher, counselor, guidance coordinator, and administrator. Recognized for her expertise in the field of character education, Dr. Gholar assisted in developing the K–12 Character Education Curriculum for the Chicago Public Schools, and she is a five-year participant in the White House Conference on Character Building for a Democratic and Civil Society. The recipient of numerous awards, she is also the author of *Beyond Rhetoric and Rainbows: A Journey to the Place Where Learning Lives.*

Ernestine G. Riggs is an Assistant Professor at Loyola University Chicago and a Senior Program Consultant for the North Central Regional Educational Laboratory. She has a Ph.D. in Educational Leadership and Policy Studies from Loyola University, and she has been involved in the field of education for more than 35 years. An advocate of teaching the whole child, she is a frequent presenter at district and national conferences; she also serves as a consultant for several state boards of education. Dr. Riggs has received many citations, including an award from the United States Department of Defense Overseas Schools for Outstanding Elementary Teacher of America.